the ABCs of YOGA for KiDS

the ABCs of YOGA for KiDS

written by
Teresa
Anne
Power

illustrated by
Kathleen
Rietz

STAFFORD HOUSE

The ABCs of Yoga for Kids
Copyright © 2009 by Teresa Anne Power

Printed in China

For information address Stafford House,
P.O. Box 291, Pacific Palisades, CA 90272.
www.staffordhousebooks.com

Publisher's Cataloging-In-Publication Data
Power, Teresa Anne.
   The ABCs of yoga for kids / written by Teresa Anne Power ; illustrated by
Kathleen Rietz. -- 1st ed.
    p. : ill. ; cm.
   ISBN: 978-0-9981070-1-1

1. Hatha yoga for children. 2. Exercise for children. 3. Yoga--Juvenile
literature. 4. Exercise--Juvenile literature. 5. Yoga. 6. Exercise. I
Rietz, Kathleen. II. Title.

RJ133.7 .P69 2009
613.7/046083   2008911816

Book Producer: Brookes Nohlgren | www.BooksByBrookes.com
Book Designer: Dotti Albertine | www.dotdesign.net

1 2 3 4 5 6 7 8 9 10
First Edition

For Trip, Kaitlyn, and Emmet.
Thank you for your love and support.

To Brookes, I couldn't have done this without you.

And to Leah, for always believing in me.
～ T.A.P.

For my sister, Anne, who is always in my corner.
～ K.R.

A a

Airplane

I am an airplane
Heading for the sky.
Lifting my chest, arms, and legs,
I begin to fly.

Alligator

Resting on my belly
A hungry alligator am I.
Open and shut go my palms
As I snap at everything nearby.

B b

Bird

High on my tiptoes,
I am a bird preparing to fly.
Flapping my wings repeatedly,
I give flying a try!

Boat

I am a sturdy boat,
Working hard to stay afloat.
First sitting up tall,
Then bending my knees,
I bring my arms
Alongside my body with ease.
Slowly lifting my legs
Up off the ground,
I like to have fun
Just steering around.

B b

Bridge

Lying on my back
And bending my knees,
I lift my hips high, forming a bridge,
And then I just breathe.
With my arms underneath me
Straight along the floor,
I press into my shoulders
And raise my body a little bit more.

Butterfly

With the soles of my feet touching,
I gaze straight ahead.
My hands rest on my shoulders,
As my butterfly wings spread.

C c

Candle

I am a candle, burning bright.
Kneeling on the floor,
I find my inner light.
My hands are in prayer position,
In front of my heart.
Breathing quietly in a yoga posture
Gives me a fresh start.

Cat

My hands and knees on the floor,
I become a cat.
Stretching one leg to form a tail,
I say, "Meow," just like that!

Chair

Standing up tall,
I bend my knees
To become a sturdy chair.
With my eyes facing front
So I can see,
I stretch both arms high in the air.

C c

Cobra

Hiss, hiss…
I am a snake,
Lying on my belly
In the sun to bake.
Elbows bent
And close by my side
I lift my chest,
Full of cobra pride.

Cow

I am a cow on all fours
Staring out the barnyard doors.
I arch my back, inhale, and say, "Moo."
Yoga is an activity I love to do.
Exhaling now, I round my spine.
This helps me keep my body aligned.

D d

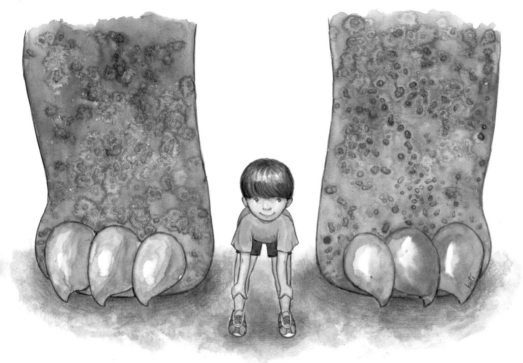

Dinosaur

The dinosaur walk is fun to do.
Anyone can do it,
Even me and you!
Standing up tall,
I slightly bend my knees.
I grab hold of my ankles
And relax at ease.
Then I walk slowly,
Lifting one leg at a time,
Knowing all the while
That I'm doing just fine.

Dog

I am a dog
Stretching from a nap.
On my hands and knees,
I begin to yap.
Straightening my legs
And lifting my hips,
I spread each and every one
Of my fingertips.
Looking down,
I can see my toes,
And I focus on breathing
In and out through my nose.

D d

Dolphin

I am a dolphin
Who loves to swim in the sea.
I sit on my heels
With my arms stretched in front of me.
Straightening my legs,
I keep my forearms on the floor.
I look at my feet
So my neck doesn't get sore.

"Do Nothing" Pose

My days can be so busy,
Sometimes it's hard
Not to get in a tizzy.
The "Do Nothing" Pose
Helps calm my mind
And keeps me from getting
Myself in a bind.
I close my eyes
And rest on my back,
Making sure that my body
Is straight—not out of whack.
With arms alongside me
And palms to the ceiling,
I focus on my breath
To keep my mind from reeling.

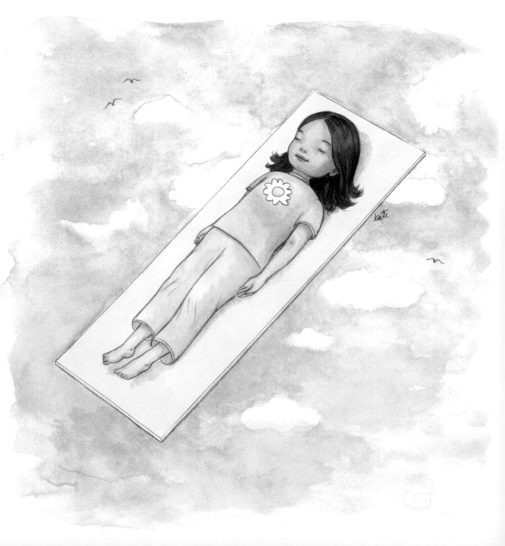

E e

Easy Pose

I like to relax in Easy Pose,
Taking deep breaths
In and out through my nose.
With my legs crossed
And my back straight,
I continue to breathe
While counting to eight.

Elephant

A mighty and powerful
Elephant am I!
From standing I fold forward
And then lumber by.
Interlacing my hands
And gently swinging my trunk,
I begin to move slowly,
Each step making a thunk.

F f

Fish

I am a fish,
Swimming deep in the sea.
Resting on my back,
I imagine the water all around me.
With my arms under my body,
I lift my chest to the ceiling.
This truly is a magnificent feeling!
With the top of my head
Resting on the ground,
I look back
Without making a sound.

Flamingo

Standing tall, I bend one leg
And hold on to my knee.
Like a flamingo I balance,
Just as stable as can be.
With my eyes focused straight ahead,
I have tremendous poise.
I hold my stance silently,
Never making a noise.
First I balance on one side,
Then switch and give the other a try.

F f

Flower

I am a beautiful flower
Growing in the sun.
Just as my teacher said it would be,
Yoga surely is fun!
Sitting with the soles
Of my feet touching,
Careful that my back
Is not hunching,
I lift my legs and bring
My arms beneath my knees.
Balancing on my seat,
I count to three.

Frog

Squatting
With my feet apart wide,
I am a frog
With a big underside.
Bringing my arms
Inside my knees,
I jump up and say,
"R-r-r-r-i-b-b-i-t!"
On the count of three.

G g

Gate

Starting on all fours,
One leg bends
While the other one extends.
Keeping my front arm straight,
My body begins to form a gate.
Sending my opposite arm up in the air,
I now balance in Gate Pose with care.

Grasshopper

In yoga, my body can be
Many different things.
Now I want to be
A grasshopper with wings!
Lying on my belly,
With my chin on the floor,
I take a moment to simply rest,
Doing nothing more.
Next I bend my arms
And raise one leg off the ground.
I bring my leg back down and switch sides,
All without a sound.

Hh Ii Jj

Happy Baby

Hugging my knees
Into my chest,
I lie on my back
And simply rest.
As I grab hold of my feet,
I look like a baby,
So happy and sweet!

Inhale

One of the most important parts
Of any yoga pose,
Is remembering to breathe deeply
By inhaling through my nose.

Jack-in-the-Box

Sitting with my knees bent into my chest,
I bring my arms around them
And take a moment to rest.
I point my forehead toward my knees
And for the count of three
I hold still—I freeze!
Then, inhaling, I lift
My head toward the sky.
Popping up, a jack-in-the-box am I!

K k

Kite

I am a colorful kite.
Standing tall,
I get ready for flight.
With palms together,
I raise my arms in the air.
Swaying gently, side to side,
I don't have a single care.

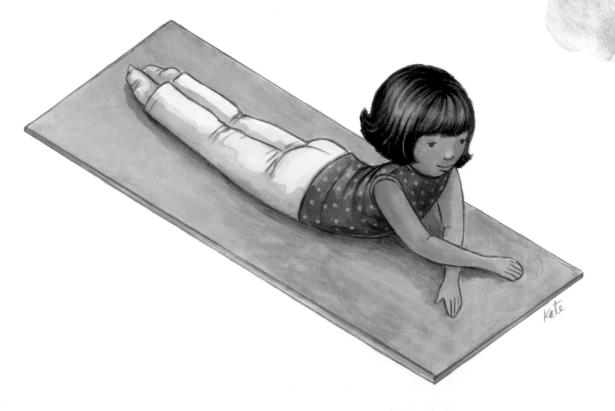

Knot

On my belly I lie.
The Knot Pose is so easy,
I hardly have to try.
With arms crossed in front of me
And legs stretched out behind,
I focus straight ahead.
What a good way to unwind!

Ll Mm Nn

Lion

I kneel on my shins
With my chest on my thighs.
Getting ready to spring forward,
I look to the sky.
I give a mighty roar
On the count of three.
The new king of the jungle,
Yes, a lion, that's me!

Mouse

I am a quiet mouse
Curled up in my little house.
I put my head on the floor
And sit back on my heels,
Then I fold my upper body some more.
Oh, I like how this feels!
I put my arms at my side.
There are so many places
For a mouse like me to hide.

New Pose

It's time for me to create
A *new* yoga pose.
I must remember to breathe
In and out through my nose!

O o

Otter

I am a playful otter,
Chasing fish in the water.
Lying on my belly
With my arms out in front,
I place my legs on the floor
And extend them from my trunk.
Slowly pushing up
With my hands against the floor,
I lift my head and chest
Just a little bit more.

P p

Peacock

I am a colorful peacock,
Sitting proud and tall.
My back is so straight,
It's like I'm sitting against a wall.
I spread my legs apart
As far as they can go,
Feeling the stretch all the way
From my head down to my toes.

Plank

My body forms a plank—a long, flat piece of timber.
Doing yoga helps my body to stay both strong and limber.
From Dog Pose, I shift my weight forward, until I'm parallel to the floor.
My arms and legs are straight as I pull up through my core.

Pretzel

A pretzel is yummy to eat.
It's a very twisty treat!
First I sit in Easy Pose,
Then turn my head to one side
And stare at my nose.
Reaching one hand across my body,
I rest it on my knee.
My other hand then stretches
Directly behind me.
Before switching sides
I count to eight.
Twisting really does feel great!

Q q

Queen

I am a royal queen,
Revered in such high esteem.
I stand tall and erect,
And make sure my
Breathing is correct.
With my shoulders back
And head facing straight,
I slowly count to eight.

R r

Rag Doll

From standing,
I lean forward and fold.
My hands dangle about
As I count to five, then hold.
I am a floppy rag doll,
Relaxed and at ease.
I breathe in and out
As I let my back release.

Rocking Horse

Lying on my belly,
Bending both of my knees,
I rock back and forth
Just as often as I please.
Grabbing hold of my ankles
With the firm grip of my hands,
I lift my body up
And gallop to far-away lands.

S s

Shark

I am a stealthy shark,
Cruising through the sea.
I lie on my belly
With my legs straight behind me.
My fingers interlace
As I lift my arms and chest.
My fin can be seen by all
As I ride a wave's crest.

Slide

To form a slippery slide,
I sit with bent knees.
Then I bring my arms
Behind me with ease.
Straightening my legs
And lifting my hips,
I gaze with eyes forward
As a smile comes to my lips.

S s

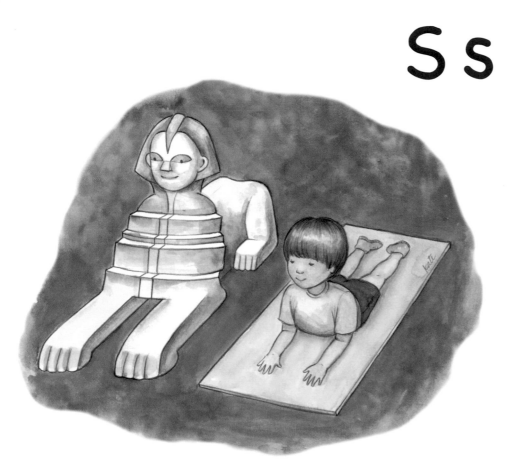

Sphinx

The Egyptian Sphinx
Is part lion and part man.
Made of stone, I lie still
On my belly in the sand.
With legs straight
And forearms pressed
Firmly into the ground,
I look forward, frozen in time,
Without making a sound.

Swan

I am a beautiful swan.
My neck is graceful and long.
Starting on my belly,
I straighten my arms
And bend my knees
Folding myself backwards,
But only as far as I please.
I aim the top of my head
In the direction of my toes,
Arching just as far
As my back naturally goes.

T t

Table

To create the shape of a table,
I must be strong and stable.
Sitting up tall
With hands behind me,
I'm as sturdy as can be.
I press into my hands
And into my feet.
Lifting my body up,
I await a healthy treat!

hello?

Telephone

Seated, I extend one leg
And then bend the other.
The Telephone Pose
Is truly like no other!
Grabbing a hold of my foot,
And bringing it close to my ear,
I can now talk on the phone
To friends both far and near.

T t

Tree

I am an old and solid tree.
My roots grow deep into the ground beneath me.
Bending one leg, I bring my foot to my thigh.
Balancing can be tricky, but I'll give it a try!
I focus my sight on a single spot.
Yoga improves my concentration a lot!

T t

Triangle

Stepping my feet wide apart
I point the toes of one foot
Straight ahead to start.
Lifting my top arm, I begin
To reach my other arm
Down toward my shin.
I breathe in and out
For the count of four
Before switching sides
And trying Triangle Pose once more.

Turtle

From a seated position,
I bend my knees and open my legs wide.
I am becoming a shy turtle,
Carrying a shell in which to hide.
With my feet flat on the floor,
I bring my arms under my knees.
Looking down toward my belly,
I count, "One-two-three!"
Then slowly lifting
My head out of my shell,
I look up and see that
The world around me is swell.

Uu Vv

Unicorn

To become a unicorn
From a far-away mythical land,
I start on my knees and on my hands.
I form a horn by lifting one hand to my head.
To maintain good balance,
I keep my eyes straight ahead.
With my other hand, I press into the floor.
The Unicorn Pose requires nothing more.

Volcano

Standing tall
With my feet slightly apart,
I bring my hands into prayer
In front of my heart.
Inhaling, I push my hands
To the sky.
The Volcano Pose
Is fun to try!
Exhaling, I explode,
Moving my arms to the side.
I then bring them
Back to center,
Where, once again,
They quietly reside.

W w

Warrior

I am a warrior,
Proud and strong.
I stand with feet wide apart
And arms extended long.
Pointing my front toes straight ahead,
I bend my front knee.
Warrior Pose is a powerful posture,
As everyone can see!

Waterfall

Raising my arms up, I stand tall.
My body forms the shape of a flowing waterfall.
As I reach my fingertips to the sky,
I look toward my hands, held up high.
Extending back as far as I can comfortably go,
I let my mind and body begin to gently flow.

W w

Windmill

Standing with legs slightly bent
And my feet wide apart,
I bring one hand down to the ground
In line with my heart.
Sending my other arm
Up toward the sky,
I extend it long
And keep reaching it high.
Switching arms
On the count of three,
I am a windmill,
Twirling and carefree.

Windshield Wipers

Lying down
With my knees at my chest,
I hold on to my legs
And take a moment to rest.
I then begin to roll
From side to side,
Just like a windshield wiper
When it's raining outside.

Xx Yy Zz

X

Standing up straight
And crossing one arm
Over the other,
I am able to create
The Letter X.
Holding still,
I count to eight.

Yoga

Yoga means "union"
Of breath, body and mind.
As you practice these poses,
You will start to find
A sense of calm and serenity,
Building deep within you
A strong and stable identity.

yoga peace Bend reach focus
Concentrate Balance calm
serenity live stretch
Breathe
hold center
clarity visualize
energy relax

Zero

Sitting cross-legged I start,
Then send my arms
Up toward the sky.
Doing the Zero Pose
Is something everyone should try.
To make the number zero,
I connect my fingers in the air.
By focusing my gaze
Straight ahead of me,
I become more aware.